To Greg
Love Always
Mom

2022

D1602312

STAND *in the* LIGHT

NATIVE VOICES ILLUMINATED BY EDWARD S. CURTIS

Compiled by Thomas F. Voight

RIO NUEVO
PUBLISHERS

Dedicated to those who keep the ceremonies, traditions, history, stories, songs, and prayers for coming generations.

Thank you for all you do.

Rio Nuevo Publishers®

P. O. Box 5250 | Tucson, AZ 85703-0250

(520) 623-9558 | www.rionuevo.com

Design by Katie Jennings Campbell

Managing Editor: Aaron Downey

Library of Congress Cataloging-in-Publication Data

Names: Curtis, Edward S., 1868-1952, photographer. | Voight, Thomas F., compiler. | Voight, Diane Christoffel, editor.
Title: Stand in the light : native voices illuminated by Edward S. Curtis / compiled by Thomas F. Voight ; edited by Diane Christoffel Voight. Description: Tucson, AZ : Rio Nuevo Publishers, [2018] | Includes bibliographical references.
Identifiers: LCCN 2018039701 | ISBN 9781940322346 (pbk.) | ISBN 1940322340 (pbk.)
Subjects: LCSH: Curtis, Edward S., 1868-1952. | Indians of North America—Pictorial works. |
Portrait prints—20th century. | Photography—United States. | Indians of North America—Literary collections.
Classification: LCC TR681.I58 C87 2018 | DDC 770.92—dc23 LC record available at https://lccn.loc.gov/2018039701

Printed in Korea.

10 9 8 7 6 5 4

CONTENTS

A NOTE ON THE TEXT

The term *American Indian* has been used for hundreds of years to identify the indigenous people of North America. It is used by institutions such as the Smithsonian's National Museum of the American Indian, the Indian Craft Shop, both located in Washington, DC; the Institute of American Indian Art, Santa Fe, NM; the Southwest Museum of the American Indian, Los Angeles, CA; as well as museums throughout the United States. This term is also used by organizations such as the American Indian College Fund, the Association on American Indian Affairs, Running Strong for American Indian Youth, and the American Indian Movement. The alternate term *Native American* came into use in the latter half of the twentieth century. Other terms also used are *Native Peoples* and *First Nations*. I believe *American Indian* has a power and strength that represents the language, culture, and tradition of these people. For this reason *American Indian* will be used respectfully throughout this book.

The names of Indian tribes and nations have also changed over the years. Some examples of tribal names that are used in this book are: Navaho, Apache, Hopi, Apsaroke, Sioux, and Nez Perce. These names are of European origin.

The name *Navajo*, given by the Spanish, means "people of the cultivated fields." *Navaho* was the popular spelling in the eighteenth and early nineteenth centuries. The spelling was changed to Navajo and is still used by the Navajo Nation. Their traditional name is *Diné*.

Apache is also a Spanish word corrupted from the Zuni *Apachu*, meaning "enemy." The Apache are made up of six divisions; Western, Chiracahua, Mescalero, Jicarilla, Lipan, and

Kiowa Apache. Their traditional name is *Inde* or *Nde*, which means "the People."

The Hopis traditional name is *Hopitu*, meaning "the Peaceful Ones."

The Zuni tribal name is *A:shiwi*.

The Apsaroke or Apsaroka are commonly known as the Crow. Their proper name is *Apsáalooke*, meaning "children of the large beaked bird."

The people known as the Sioux were given that name by French fur traders. They call themselves *Oceti Sakowin*, Seven Council Fires. There are seven divisions of what is known as "the Great Sioux Nation." The number seven is from their creation story. To the Sioux, the stars of the Big Dipper signify the Seven Council Fires.

The traditional name of the Nez Perce people is *Nimiipuu*, meaning "the People." *Nez Perce* was the name given to them by French fur traders and means "pierced noses." The Nimiipuu never pierced their noses, but the French confused them with the neighboring Chinook Tribe who did.

The songs, prayers, and proverbs included in this book are meant to give voice to Edward Curtis's photographs. In the case of songs, some were edited due to their length or repetition of stanzas. The idea was to use a specific part of a song or verse that complements the photograph. The exception is *A Monthly Offering of Prayer Sticks* in the Zuni chapter. That entire prayer with different photographs is shown to give the reader a perception of the harmony of Zuni people, culture, and religion. Complete songs and prayers can be found in books included in the bibliography.

The descriptions accompanying some of the photographs are from Edward S. Curtis's book, *The North American Indian*. Most are descriptions Curtis made of the specific photograph. Some are descriptions from the text and are used as they fit the subject. To bring authenticity to this book, Curtis's quotes and titles are used in their original form, verbatim and unedited. One exception is the "American Horse" page with a description by Ohiyesa, a Santee Dakota.

The songs and prayers are also translated from the original native languages to English, so there are certain considerations. Should an ethnologist or anthropologist approach an individual to record a song, the singer is giving his or her interpretation. The song is then translated either by the singer or a tribal member. The scholar then writes down the literal translation, after which the scholar may decide to add, subtract, or rearrange words for either a more dramatic effect or to make it easier to enjoy in the English language. There is also the possibility that another scholar records another singer of the same song. That singer uses different words or nuances, singing the same song. Most important, many of these songs and prayers are sacred. The tribal member may change or omit certain stanzas or sentences to prevent nontribal members from misusing them.

In the introduction of the appendix to *The Indians' Book: Songs and Legends of the American Indians*, Natalie Curtis writes: "The interlinear translations here given have been made with care in the hope that the book may be of some aid in the comparative study of the linguistic stocks of the North American continent; yet they are offered as approximate only, for philological accuracy requires full and intimate knowledge of Indian languages—a knowledge which the recorder does not possess. . . . The words in Indian songs are often changed for euphony in singing, or they are prolonged for rhythmic and poetic effect by the addition of vocables. In the following pages the aim has been to present only actual words, omitting vocables and meaningless refrains."

Also, the translations of names and greetings are often changed to fit the English language. The name of a Tewa maiden is Povi-Tamu, literally "Flower Morning." The correct interpretation would be "Flower of the Morning," which ends up becoming "Morning Flower." The Lakota "Paha Sapa" is "Hills Black," which becomes "Hills that are Black," or in English, "Black Hills."

Finally, the translations themselves are using words from the later nineteenth and early twentieth century. Words like *saith, there of, telleth, hither,* and *o'er* are not in use in the twenty-first century and would be translated and interpreted differently today.

If we are to keep things in historical context, it should be understood that the presentation of songs and prayers in the book, while there may be different interpretations, preserve and respect their meaning.

This book is meant to be a positive presentation of American Indian culture. I hope you find it inspirational and it becomes part of your life.

Edward S. Curtis, 1899

INTRODUCTION

"The passing of every old man or woman means the passing of some tradition, some knowledge of sacred rites possessed by no other; consequently the information to be gathered, for the benefit of future generations, respecting the mode of life of one of the great races of mankind, must be collected at once or the opportunity will be lost for all time. It is this need that has inspired the present task." —Edward S. Curtis

Beautiful Pictures

The beautiful historical pictures included in this book are by the photogravure artist Edward Sheriff Curtis. While there were many photographs taken of American Indians beginning in the 1860s, very few match Curtis's quality and beauty. Photographs of American Indians in the latter half of the nineteenth century were typically of tribal delegations or important leaders visiting Washington, D.C. Also popular were portraits taken in a studio, scenes of treaty signings, and pictures of ceremonies in villages of a specific tribe. There were some photographers who traveled with military or scientific expeditions and others who photographed multiple tribes. Frank A. Rinehart visited reservations over a two-year period and was the official photographer for the Trans-Mississippi and International Exposition held in Omaha,

Nebraska, in 1898. David Barry photographed military forts, battlefields, pioneers, and western personalities such as Sitting Bull, Red Cloud, and Buffalo Bill. Roland Reed photographed tribes of the northern plains and the great southwest, as well as the Ojibwa of Minnesota. All three of these men have some outstanding and beautiful photographs, but none of them could have conceived of the momentous undertaking to which Curtis devoted himself.

Princess Angeline, 1896
Daughter of Chief Seattle

Curtis had a successful portrait studio in Seattle when he began spending time in the surrounding area photographing mountains, lakes, and landscapes. His interest in American Indians as a subject began in 1896 when he photographed Princess Angeline, the daughter of the Duwamish-Suquamish Chief Seattle. She was impressed with his sincere interest in her and her tribal history and customs. She directed him to where Duwamish people were living outside the city. They in turn told him of the Tulalip tribe living to the north. Soon Curtis found an admiration and respect for the Tulalip people and wanted to capture their daily activities as well as portraits of individuals.

Then, in 1898 while hiking Mount Rainier, he came upon a group of men who were lost. He offered to guide them and when introductions were made, he was astonished to find they were prominent scholars in the fields of science and ethnology. C. Hart Merriam was one of the original founders of the National Geographic Society, a distinguished botanist, ornithologist, zoologist, and author. George Bird Grinnell was an anthropologist, historian, the naturalist on the Black Hills Expedition of 1874, founder of the Audubon Society, and a historian of Plains Indians. He had already published books on the Pawnee, Plains Indians, and the Blackfeet. He was adopted into the Blackfeet Tribe in 1885 and published *Blackfoot Lodge Tales* in 1892. They were impressed as they listened to the enthusiasm and passion Curtis had for preserving the history and culture of the American Indian. They also thought it admirable that a young man who had dropped out of school before he was twelve years old could take such beautiful pictures and express himself so well.

Industrialist and railroad tycoon, E. H. Harriman, invited Curtis to be the official photographer of his scientific expedition to Alaska in 1899. In 1900 he met Grinnell in Montana and was introduced to the Blackfeet tribe. Curtis was impressed by Grinnell's respect for the Blackfeet and their ways. As a friend of Grinnell, Curtis was invited into the sweat lodge and to witness ceremonies and record stories. Later, after fees were negotiated, he was allowed to take photographs.

Returning from Montana, Curtis made arrangements with his wife and employees to take care of the studio in his absence. That summer of 1900, Curtis boarded a train for Arizona. He would begin *The North American Indian* project by photographing the Hopi and Navajo. In the general introduction of Volume 1, published in 1907, Curtis explained his ultimate goal:

> It has been the aim to picture all features of the Indian life and environment—types of the young and old, with their habitations, industries, ceremonies, games, and everyday customs. Rather than being designed for mere embellishment, the photographs are each an illustration of an Indian character or of some vital phase in his existence. Yet the fact that the Indian and his surroundings lend themselves to artistic treatment has not been lost sight of, for in his country one may treat limitless subjects of an aesthetic character without in any way doing injustice to scientific accuracy or neglecting the homelier phases of aboriginal life. Indeed, in a work of this sort, to overlook those marvelous touches that Nature has given to the Indian country, and for the origin of which the native ever has a wonder-tale to relate, would be to neglect a most important chapter in the story of an environment that made the Indian much of what he is. Therefore, being directly from Nature, the accompanying pictures show what actually exists or has recently existed (for many of the subjects have already passed forever), not what the artist in his studio may presume the Indian and his surroundings to be.

In this endeavor, Edward Curtis succeeded as no other could have ever hoped to. Between 1900 and 1927, Curtis would visit eighty different tribes, traveling from the U.S.-Mexico border to the Arctic Circle, from the Great Plains to the Pacific Coast. He would take over 40,000 photographs, record songs and stories, interview famous tribal leaders, and produce a full-length silent film of the Kwakiutl people. He exhausted his personal funds and secured financial backing from J. P. Morgan. The expenses far outweighed what little income he made selling individual photographs. He lost his studio, his wife divorced him, and he was forced to declare bankruptcy. But he persevered. By 1930 he had completed and published all 20 volumes of *The North American Indian*.

The importance of *The North American Indian* is still not fully appreciated. The text, written by Curtis with assistance from William Myers and Bill Phillips, was edited by Frederick Hodges, who is still recognized as a preeminent scholar in American Indian studies. The interviews Curtis conducted with individuals give incredible insight into their lives. His biographical sketches and personal observations of ceremonies and daily life of American Indians are unequalled. While the photographs are beautiful and works of art, they also serve a greater purpose. They allow American Indians of today to look back on a way of life their ancestors experienced, as well as give some of them the ability to see pictures of their relatives that would have been nonexistent if not for Edward S. Curtis.

Beautiful Words

Beautiful words are the prayers, songs, and wisdom of the American Indian tribes included in this book. They give voice to the artistic photographs of Edward Curtis. Each chapter features photographs and verses of a specific tribe.

The American Indians lived in harmony with their environment and gave homage to the Great Spirit. Individual prayers would begin each day, often with an offering of tobacco, corn meal, or medicine. Prayer ties, prayer sticks, and prayer wands or feathers could also be used to carry prayers to the Creator. The appearance of an eagle was considered a good omen, as the eagle is seen as a messenger and mediator between man and the Great Spirit. The magic, power, and blessings of the Creator are a constant presence. In the natural world, animals, plants, water, wind, and earth are all part of the spirit world. The Dakota expression, Mitakuye Oyasin (we are all related), refers not only to people but also Mother Earth, Father Sky, the sun, and stars.

> The elements and majestic forces in nature, Lightning, Wind, Water, Fire and Frost, were regarded with awe as spiritual powers, but always secondary and intermediate in character. We believed that the spirit pervades all creation and that every creature possesses a soul in some degree, though not necessarily a soul conscious of itself. The tree, the waterfall, the grizzly bear, each is an embodied Force, and as such an object of reverence.
>
> —Dr. Charles A. Eastman (Ohiyesa), Santee Dakota, from *The Soul Of The Indian: An Interpretation*

Songs are a very important part of American Indian culture. The singers not only preserve traditional songs but also compose individual and contemporary songs. Traditional songs include healing, sweat lodge, religious, social dance songs, and lullabies. Individuals may have personal magic, story, or war songs. Ceremonial songs, such as medicine songs and religious dance songs, are taught from generation to generation. Contemporary songs include powwow, love, and social commentary songs. Good singers are still very popular and invited to ceremonies and powwows. Men and women who sing with a strong voice combined with emotional feeling are greatly admired. Singers can create a personal song that tells of an important deed or a vision that gives them power. In *The Indians' Book*, Geronimo related to Natalie Curtis, the editor, the origin and importance of his song before singing it for her.

> The song that I will sing is an old song, so old that none knows who made it.
> It has been handed down through generations and was taught to me when
> I was but a little lad. It is now my own song. It belongs to me. This is a holy
> song and great is its power. The song tells how, as I sing, I go through the air
> to a holy place where Yuson will give me power to do wonderful things. I am
> surrounded by little clouds, and as I go through the air I change and become
> spirit only.

O, ha le

O, ha le!

Through the air

I fly upon a cloud

Towards the sky, far, far, far,

O, ha le

O, ha le!

There to find the holy place

Ah, now the change comes o'er me!

O, ha le

O, ha le!

—Geronimo's Holy Song

    Wisdom comes from teachings through stories and instruction. From father to son, mother to daughter, and grandparents to grandchildren, ancient stories are handed down through generations. The same story may be told many times so the listener understands the significance of each detail. Oral history is very important because stories are kept with the people. The young people must go to the elders to learn these stories so they are not lost. The stories give the next generation a strength and pride in their heritage. They teach traditional and moral values, as well as legends and tribal history. Children learned proper behavior and duties to be performed by accompanying the elders on a daily basis.

> In Lakota society it was the duty of every parent to give the knowledge they possessed to their children. Each and every parent was a teacher and, as a matter of fact, all elders were instructors of those younger than themselves. And the instruction they gave was mostly through their actions—that is, they interpreted to us through actions what we should try to do. We learned by watching and imitating examples placed before us. Slowly and naturally the faculties of observation and memory became highly trained and the Lakota child became educated in the manners, lore, and customs of his people without a strained and conscious effort.

> —Luther Standing Bear, from *Land Of The Spotted Eagle*

May the words in this collection give the reader a respect and understanding for the philosophy and ideals of these tribal cultures and an appreciation for their love of the natural world.

Navaho Still Life, 1907

The
NAVAJO

The Vanishing Race. 1904

"THE THOUGHT WHICH THIS PICTURE IS MEANT TO CONVEY is that the Indians as a race, already shorn of their tribal strength and stripped of their primitive dress, are passing into the darkness of an unknown future. Feeling that the picture expresses so much of the thought that inspired the entire work, the author has chosen it as the first of the series." —ESC

To the house of my kindred,
>*There I return.*
Child of the yellow corn am I.
To the Red Rock House,
>*There I return.*
Where the blue kethawns are by the doorway,
>*There I return.*
The pollen of evening light on my trail,
>*There I return.*
At the yuni the haliotis shell hangs with the pollen,
Going around,
>*With it I return.*
Taking another, I walk out with it.
>*With it I return.*
To the house of old age,
>*Up there I return.*
To the house of happiness,
>*Up there I return.*
Beauty behind me,
>*With it I return.*
Beauty before me,
>*With it I return.*
Beauty above me,
>*With it I return.*
Beauty below me,
>*With it I return.*
Beauty all around me,
>*With it I return.*
Now in old age wandering,
>*I return.*
Now on the trail of beauty, I am.
>*There I return.*

—From *Third Song of Dawn Boy*

"A WONDERFULLY SCENIC SPOT is this in northeastern Arizona, in the heart of the Navaho country—one of their strongholds, in fact. Cañon de Chelly exhibits evidence of having been occupied by a considerable number of people in former times, as in every niche at every side are seen the cliff-perched ruins of former villages." —ESC

May their roads home be on the trail of peace.
Happily may they all return.
In beauty I walk.
With beauty before me, I walk.
With beauty behind me, I walk.
With beauty above and about me, I walk.
It is finished in beauty,
It is finished in beauty.

—From *Night Chant, for the ninth song*

Cañon de Chelly, 1904

Blanket Weaver, 1904

"THE NAVAHO-LAND BLANKET LOOMS are in evidence everywhere. In the winter months they are set up in the hogans, but during the summer they are erected outdoors under an improvised shelter, or, as in this case, beneath a tree. The simplicity of the loom and its product are here clearly shown, pictured in the early morning light under a large cottonwood." —ESC

May You Walk in Beauty
On a Rainbow Trail
And Dwell in
The House Of Happiness
With Beauty All Around You.

—From a Navajo blessing

The Earth is looking at me; she is looking
  up at me
I am looking down on her
I am happy, she is looking at me
I am happy, I am looking at her.

The Sun is looking at me; he is looking
  down on me
I am looking up at him
I am happy, he is looking at me
I am happy, I am looking at him.

The Black Sky is looking at me; he is
  looking down on me
I am looking up at him
I am happy, he is looking at me
I am happy, I am looking at him.

The Moon is looking at me; he is looking
  down on me
I am looking up at him.
I am happy, he is looking at me.
I am happy, I am looking at him.

The North is looking at me; he is looking
  across at me
I am looking across at him
I am happy, he is looking at me
I am happy, I am looking at him.

—Navajo chant from the origin legend,
  When They Saw Each Other

Nature's Mirror, 1904

Hastobiga — Navajo Medicine Man, 1904

It is lovely indeed, it is lovely indeed.
I, I am the spirit within the earth.
The feet of the earth are my feet,
The legs of the earth are my legs,
The bodily strength of the earth, is my strength.
The thoughts of the earth are my thoughts,
The voice of the earth is my voice.
The feather of the earth is my feather.
All that belongs to the earth belongs to me,
All that surrounds the earth surrounds me.
I, I am the sacred words of the earth
It is lovely indeed, it is lovely indeed.

—*Song of the Earth Spirit*

"A WELL-KNOWN NAVAHO MEDICINE-MAN. While in the Cañon de Chelly the writer witnessed a very interesting four days' ceremony given by the Wind Doctor." —ESC

Where my kindred dwell, there I wander.
The Red Rock House, there I wander
Where dark kethawns are at the doorway, there I wander.
With the pollen of dawn upon my trail, there I wander.
At the yuni, the striped cotton hangs with pollen. There I wander.
Going around with it. There I wander.
Taking another, I depart with it. With it I wander.
In the house of long life, there I wander.
In the house of happiness, there I wander.
Beauty before me, with it I wander.
Beauty behind me, with it I wander.
Beauty below me, with it I wander.
Beauty above me, with it I wander.
Beauty all around me, with it I wander.
In old age traveling, with it I wander.
On the beautiful trail I am, with it I wander.

—From *Songs of Dawn Boy, First Song*

Nesjaja Hatali, 1904

A Navaho Smile, 1904

Today I will walk out,
Today everything evil will leave me,
I will be as I was before,
I will have a cool breeze over my body,
I will walk with a light body.

I will be happy forever, nothing will hinder me.
I walk with beauty before me,
I walk with beauty behind me,
I walk with beauty below me,
I walk with beauty above me,
I walk with beauty around me.
My words will be beautiful.

—*Myth of the Beauty Way,* female Navajo prayer

"IN THE EARLY MORNING THIS BOY, as if springing from the earth itself, came to the author's desert camp. Indeed, he seemed a part of the very desert. His eyes bespeak all the curiosity, all the wonder of his primitive mind striving to grasp the meaning of the strange things about him." —ESC

Dewdrops and pollens
may I enjoy.
With these may it be
beautiful in front of me.
With these may it be
beautiful behind me.
All is beautiful again.
All is restored in beauty.

—From *Male Shooting Way* chant

Son of the Desert, 1904

Women of the Desert, 1906

"THE NAVAHO WOMEN are, for the greater part, the owners of the flocks and invariably, with the children, the herders. They are so thoroughly at home on their scrubby ponies that they seem a part of them and probably excel all other Indians as horsewomen." —ESC

All is beautiful,
All is beautiful,
All is beautiful indeed.
   Now the Mother Earth, And the
   Father Sky,
Meeting, joining one another, helpmates
   ever, they.
All is beautiful,
All is beautiful,
All is beautiful indeed.

   . . .

And the night of darkness, And the dawn
   of light,
Meeting, joining one another, helpmates
   ever, they.

All is beautiful,
All is beautiful,
All is beautiful indeed.

   . . .

Life that never passes, Happiness of
   all things.
Meeting, joining one another, helpmates
   ever, they.
All is beautiful,
All is beautiful,
All is beautiful indeed.

Now all is beautiful,
All is beautiful,
All is beautiful indeed.

—From *Song of the Earth*

From meadows green where ponds are scattered,
From there we come.
Bereft of limbs, one bears another,
From there we come.
Bereft of eyes, one bears another,
From there we come.
By ponds where healing herbs are growing,
From there we come.
With these your limbs you shall recover,
From there we come.
With these your eyes you shall recover,
From there we come.

—From *Song of the Stricken Twins, Navajo Night Way Myth*

A Point of Interest, 1904

A Drink in the Desert, 1904

I am the Turquoise Woman's son

On top of Belted Mountain beautiful horses
   slim like a weasel

My horse has a hoof like striped agate
his fetlock is like fine eagle plume
his legs are like quick lightning

My horse's body is like an eagle-feathered arrow

My horse has a tail like a trailing black cloud

I put flexible goods on my horse's back

The Holy Wind blows through his mane
his mane is made of rainbows

My horse's ears are made of round corn

My horse's eyes are made of stars

My horse's head is made of mixed waters
   (from the holy waters)

(he never knows thirst)
My horse's teeth are made of white shell

The long rainbow is in his mouth for a bridle
with it I guide him

When my horse neighs different-colored
   horses follow

When my horse neighs different-colored
   sheep follow

I am wealthy from my horse

Before me peaceful
Behind me peaceful
Under me peaceful
Over me peaceful
Around me peaceful
Peaceful voice when he neighs
I am everlasting and peaceful
I stand for my horse

—From *War God's Horse Song*

X1920-06

Storm, 1906

The
APACHE

The Apache, 1906

In this world,
the unseen has power.

—Apache wisdom

"CHIEF OF THE WHITE MOUNTAIN APACHE. A well-known character, having been a scout with General Crook. Colonel Cooley, who was chief of scouts under Crook, says a braver man than Alchise never lived. He was about twenty-two when Fort Apache, then Camp Ord, was established in 1870, making the year of his birth about 1848." —ESC

It is senseless to fight
when you cannot hope to win.

—Geronimo

X1914-06

Alchise, 1906

Apache Babe in Carrier, 1903

"A FORTUNATE CHILD PICTURE, giving a good idea of the happy disposition of Indian children, and at the same time, showing the baby carrier or holder." —ESC

Childhood is the best
season of your life.

—Apache proverb

It makes no difference
as to the name of the God,
since Love is the real god
of all the world.

—Apache wisdom

X1906-06

Mizheh and Babe, 1906

Sigesh, 1903

"THIS ILLUSTRATES THE GIRLS' METHOD of tying the hair previous to marriage. The ornament fastened to the hair in the back is made of leather, broad and round at the ends and narrow in the middle." —ESC

Even your silence
holds a sort of prayer.

—Apache wisdom

You must speak straight
so that your words may go
as sunlight into our hearts.

—Cochise, Chiricahua Apache

Tsahizn Tseh, 1906

Geronimo, 1905

"THIS PORTRAIT OF THE HISTORICAL OLD APACHE was made in March, 1905. According to Geronimo's calculation he was at the time seventy-six years of age, thus making the year of his birth 1829. The picture was taken at Carlisle, Pennsylvania, the day before the inauguration of President [Theodore] Roosevelt, Geronimo being one of the warriors who took part in the inaugural parade at Washington. He appreciated the honor of being one of those chosen for this occasion, and the catching of his features while the old warrior was in a retrospective mood was most fortunate." —ESC

"I cannot think that we are useless
or God would not have created us.
There is one God looking down on us all.
We are all children of one God.
The sun, the darkness, the winds are all
listening to what we have to say."

—Geronimo, Bedonkohe Apache

East Mesa Pottery, 1921

The
HOPI

East Side of Walpi, 1921

"FEW ILLUSTRATIONS OF HOPI ARCHITECTURE show as much regularity as this view of a Walpi street." —ESC

The Supreme law of the land
is the Great Spirit's law,
not man's law.

—Hopi wisdom

"PICTURESQUE WALPI, perched on the point of a rocky island in a sea of sand, is an irregular, rambling community-house, built without design, added to in haphazard fashion as need arose, yet it constitutes a perfectly satisfying artistic whole." —ESC

Yellow butterflies,
Over the blossoming virgin corn,
With pollen-painted faces,
Chase one another in brilliant throng.

Blue butterflies,
Over the blossoming virgin beans,
With pollen-painted faces,
Chase one another in brilliant streams.

Over the blossoming corn,
Over the virgin corn,
Wild bees hum!

Over the blossoming beans,
Over the virgin beans,
Wild bees hum!

Over your field of growing corn
All day shall hang the thunder-cloud;.
Over your field of growing corn
All day shall come the rushing rain.

—Korosta katsina song

Walpi, 1907

Hopi Girls in Window, 1900

Take a breath
of the new dawn
and make it a part of you.

—Hopi wisdom

"AFFABILITY AND SUNNY DISPOSITION are apt to be one's first impression of the dominating traits of Hopi character. . . . Presume on this affability, and you encounter cold reserve, ill-concealed disapproval, or outspoken resentment." —ESC

Thus we, thus we,
The night along,
With happy hearts
Wish well one another.

In the chief's kiva
They, the fathers
They, and Muyingwa
Plant the double ear—

Plant the perfect double corn-ear.
So the fields shall shine
With tassels white of perfect corn-ears.

Hither to them, hither come,
Rain that stands and cloud that rushes!

—Hopi Wuwuchim chant composed and sung
  by Lololomai

A Visitor, 1921

Potter, 1906

"EVERY VISITOR AT EAST MESA knows Nampeyo, the potter of Hano, whose creations excel those of any rival. Strangers wander into her house, welcome though unbidden, but Nampeyo only works and smiles. In the plate her paint-stone occupies the central foreground." —ESC

What should it matter
that one bowl is dark
and the other pale,
if each is of good design
and serves its purpose well?

— Polingaysi Qoyawayma (Elizabeth Q. White)

"PIKI IS CORNBREAD baked in colored sheets of paper-like thinness. The batter is spread on the baking stone with the bare hand and the quickly baked sheet is folded and laid on the basket at the baker's left." —ESC

All things have inner meaning
and form
and power.

—Hopi wisdom

The Piki Maker, 1906

Grinding Meal, 1907

"THE PRINCIPLE ARTICLES OF FURNITURE IN A HOPI HOUSE are mealing stones, earthen pots and water-jars, basketry trays, and bedding. The mealing stones are a series of three flat slabs of sandstone about fifteen inches square, cemented at a convenient angle for the worker in three compartments on the floor. They are of different degrees of fineness. On the coarsest stone the corn is crushed by rubbing with a basalt or lava muller; on the second the fragments are reduced to coarse meal with a sandstone muller; and in the third compartment a muller of still closer texture produces a meal almost as fine as our wheat flour. Girls and young women grind the corn, kneeling on the floor and working with the movement of a woman at her washboard. The work is generally performed in the morning to the accompaniment of grinding songs." —ESC

Work hard, keep the ceremonies,
live peaceably,
and unite your hearts.

—Hopi wisdom

"A GROUP OF WALPI AND HANO GIRLS in holiday attire. The background is a typical bit of Southwestern desert." —ESC

The Rainbow is a sign
from Him who is in all things.

—Hopi proverb

Loitering at the Spring, 1921

At the Trysting Place, 1921

Corn-blossom maidens,
Here in the fields,
Patches of beans in flower,
Fields all abloom,
Water shining after rain,
Blue clouds looming above.

Now behold!
Through bright clusters of flowers
Yellow butterflies are chasing at play,
And through the blossoming beans
Blue butterflies
Are chasing at play.

—He-hea katsina song

"SOFT, REGULAR FEATURES are characteristic of Hopi young women, and no small part of a mother's time is used to be devoted to dressing the hair of her unmarried daughters. The aboriginal style is rapidly being abandoned, and the native one-piece dress here illustrated is seldom seen." —ESC

Hold fast
to the words
of your ancestors.

—Hopi wisdom

Hopi Girl, 1905

Do not be afraid to cry.
It will free your mind
of sorrowful thoughts.

—Hopi wisdom

Take your children
with you where you go
and do not be ashamed.

—Hopi teaching

Hopi Angel, 1905

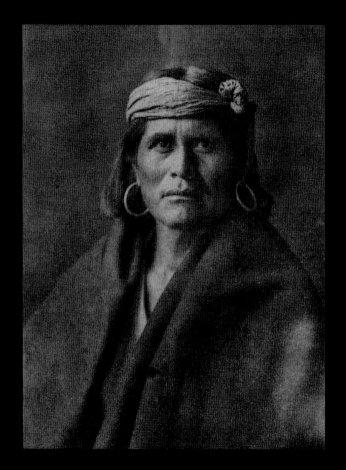

Walpi Man, 1921

Wisdom comes
when you stop looking for it
and start living the life
the Creator intended for you.

—Hopi wisdom

On the Rio Grande—San Ildefonso. 1905

The
TEWA PUEBLO

Gossiping—San Juan, 1905

Ones of the Northern Lake
Corn-Silk-Women ye are.
And now ye come to us!

Then lay long life at once upon us,
And upon our children
The love of all the gods!

May our children have many children
And our girls of San Juan live long!

And now we seek to hear
The Corn-Silk-Women say
Such words as we have said!

Long life now we ask,
And to be loved,
And to rear many children,
And to be given kindly fates!

—The Corn-Silk-Women's song

"THE FLOWER CONCEPT is a favorite one in Tewa names, both masculine and feminine." —ESC

Over there in your fields you have
Musk-melon flowers in the morning.
Over there in your fields you have
Corn-tassel flowers in the morning.
In your fields now the water bird sings
And here in your village the fogs
And the black clouds come massing.
They come here to see! They come here to see!

—*Rains For The Harvest,* Tewa song

Povi-Tamu ("Flower Morning")
—San Ildefonso, 1925

Okuwa-tse ("Cloud Yellow")
—San Ildefonso, 1905

Potter—Santa Clara, 1905

"AMONG THE VALUED GIFTS OF THE EARLY SPANISH PRIESTS was the peach. Every Pueblo has its orchards of scrubby, twisted trees, which without cultivation yield fruit of small size but agreeable flavor." —ESC

Oh, Summer Leaf! Our old man,
Now I bring you fruits
From our weary labors.
Then eat and being strong
Give food again to us.

—*When The First Fruits Are Taken*, Tewa song

Fruit Gatherer — San Ildefonso. 1905.

Okuwa-tsire — "Cloud Bird"
— San Ildefonso, 1905

In the north the cloud flower blossoms,
And now the lightning flashes,
And now the thunder clashes,
And now the rain comes down!
A-a-aha, a-a-aha, my little one.

In the west the cloud flower blossoms,
And now the lightning flashes,
And now the thunder clashes,
And now the rain comes down!
A-a-aha, a-a-aha, my little one.

In the south the cloud flower blossoms,
And now the lightning flashes,
And now the thunder clashes,
And now the rain comes down!
A-a-aha, a-a-aha, my little one.

In the east the cloud flower blossoms,
And now lightning begins to flash,
And now the thunder it thunders,
And now the rain comes down!
A-a-aha, a-a-aha, my little one.

—*The Cloud Flower Lullaby*
   Prettily we wear flowers.

Little flowers of the muskmelon we wear,
Little flowers of the watermelon we wear,
So now we wear flowers.

—*Children's Flower Song of Nambe*

Offering—San Ildefonso, 1925

"A PINCH OF CORNMEAL tossed into the air as an offering to the numerous deities of the Tewa, but especially to the sun, is a formality that begins the day and precedes innumerable acts of the most commonplace nature." —ESC

Oh our Mother the Earth, oh our Father the Sky,
Your children are we, and with tired backs
We bring you the gifts that you love.
Then weave for us a garment of brightness;
May the warp be the white light of morning,
May the weft be the red light of evening,
May the fringes be the falling rain,
May the border be the standing rainbow.
Thus weave for us a garment of brightness
That we may walk fittingly where birds sing.
That we may walk fittingly where grass is green.
Oh our Mother the Earth, oh our Father the Sky!

—*Song Of The Sky Loom*, Tewa

Zuñi Pottery, 1925

The
ZUNI

Zuñi, 1903

A Monthly Offering of Prayer Sticks

This many are the days
Since our moon mother,
Yonder in the west
Appeared still small.
When she became fully grown
Seeking yonder along the river courses
The ones who are our fathers.
Male willow,
Female willow,
Four times cutting the straight young shoots,
To my house
I brought my road.

(continues)

This day,
With my warm human hands
I took hold of them.
I gave my plume wands human form
With the striped cloud tail
Of the one who is my grandfather,
The male turkey
With the eagle's thin cloud tail,
With the striped cloud wings
And massed cloud tails
Of all the birds of summer,
With these four times I gave my plume wands human form.

(continues)

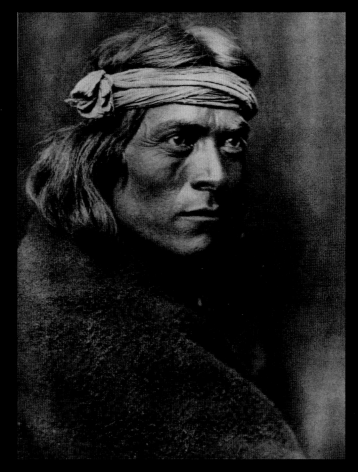

Zuñi Governor, 1925

Zuñi Girl, 1903

With the flesh of the one who is my mother,

Cotton woman,

Even a poorly made cotton thread,

Four times encircling them and tying it about their bodies,

I gave the plume wands human form.

(continues)

"THE CHAMBER AT THE LEFT, with ladder-poles projecting from the hatchway, is the kiva of the north. Many dances are performed in the small plaza here shown. The dark material piled against one of the houses is sheep-dung for firing pottery." —ESC

With the flesh of the one who is our mother,
Black paint woman,
Four times covering them with flesh,
I gave my plume wands human form.
In a short time the plume wands were ready.
Taking the plume wands,
I made my road go forth.
Yonder with prayers
We took our road.
Thinking "Let it be here,"
Our earth mother

We passed upon her road.
Our fathers,
There on your earth mother,
There where you are waiting your plume wands
We have passed you on your roads.
There where you are all gathered together
     in beauty
Now that you are to receive your plume wands,
You are gathered together.

(continues)

Corner of Zuñi, 1903

Zuñi Water Carriers, 1903

This day I give you plume wands.
By means of your supernatural wisdom
You will clothe yourself with plume wands.
Wherever you abide permanently,
At the place of the first beginning,
Touching one another with your plume wands,
You will bend down to talk together.
From where you abide permanently,
Your little wind-blown cloud,
Your thin wisps of cloud,
Your hanging stripes of clouds,
Your massed up clouds, replete with
    living waters,

You will send forth to stay with us.
They will come out standing on all sides.
With your fine rain caressing the earth.
With your weapons, the lightning,
With your rumbling thunder,
Your great crashes of thunder,
With your fine rain caressing the earth,
Your heavy rain caressing the earth,
With your great piles of water here at Itiwana,
With these you will pass us on our roads.

(continues)

In order that you may come to us thus
I have given you plume wands.

My fathers,
When you have taken your plume wands,
With your waters,
Your seeds,
Your riches,
Your power,
Your strong spirit,
Will all your good fortune whereof you are
    possessed,
Me you will bless.

(Corn meal is then sprinkled on the prayer
sticks with the following prayer):

This day, my Fathers,
I have given you plume wands.
The source of our water of life.
The source of our flesh,
Flesh of the white corn, Prayer meal I give
    you.
Taking your plume wand, Your prayer meal,
With your waters,
Your seeds,
Your riches,
Your long life,
Your old age,
With all your good fortune You will bless us.
This is all.

A Zuñi Girl, 1903

Zuñi Girls, 1903

My children,
Verily, so long as we enjoy the light of day,
We shall greet one another as kindred.

Verily, we shall pray that our roads may be
   fulfilled.
To where your sun father's road comes out
May your roads reach.
May your roads be fulfilled.

—From a Night Chant, Zuñi

Apsaroke Camp, 1908

The
APSAROKE

For a Winter Campaign, 1908

"IT WAS NOT UNCOMMON for Apsaroke war-parties, mounted or afoot, to move against the enemy in the depth of winter. . . . The warrior at the left wears the hooded overcoat of heavy blanket material that was generally adopted by the Apsaroke after the arrival of traders among them. The picture was made in a narrow valley among the Pryor Mountains, Montana." —ESC

The only things that need
the protection of man
are the things of man,
not the things of the Spirit

—Apsaroke wisdom

"DOES EVERYTHING. Born 1861. Mountain Crow; Not Mixed clan; Fox organization. When only eighteen or twenty years of age he captured a gun, struck second dákshè, and killed two Piegan in one fight, thus receiving his name. Later he took two horses from the enemy's camp." —ESC

One has to face fear
or forever run from it.

—Apsaroke wisdom

Does Everything, 1908

Apsaroke War-Chief, 1908

"THE THREE FOX-TAILS hanging from the coup-stick show the subject—Medicine Crow—to be possessor of three first coups, that is, in three encounters he was the first to strike one of the enemy's force. The necklace consists of beads, and the large ornaments at the shoulders are abalone shells." —ESC

Old age
is not as honorable
as death,
but most people
want it.

—Two Leggings

The more you give,
The more good things
come to you.

—Apsaroke wisdom

Mother and Child, 1908

Coups Well-Known, 1908

The eyes of living men
speak words
which the tongue
cannot pronounce.

—Apsaroke wisdom

Stand in the light
when you want
to speak out.

—Apsaroke wisdom

Bird on the Ground, 1908

A Smoke, 1905

Man's law changes
with his understanding of man,
only the laws of the Spirit
remain always the same.

—Apsaroke wisdom

You already possess
Everything necessary
To become great

—Apsaroke wisdom

Shot in the Hand, 1908

Oglala War Party, 1907

The
SIOUX

In the Badlands, 1904

"THIS STRIKING PICTURE was made at Sheep Mountain in the Bad Lands of Pine Ridge Indian reservation, South Dakota." —ESC

Oh, Great Spirit, Whose voice I hear in the winds,
And whose breath gives life to all the world,
Hear me. I come to you as one of your many children.
I am small and weak.
I need your strength and wisdom.
Let me walk in beauty and make my eyes ever behold the red and purple sunset.
Make my hands respect the things you have made and my ears sharp to hear your voice.
Make me wise, so that I may understand the things you have taught my people.
Let me learn the lessons you have hidden in every leaf and rock.
I seek strength, not to be greater than my brother, but to fight my greatest enemy—myself.
Make me always ready to come to you with clean hands and straight eyes.
So when life fades, as the fading sunset, my Spirit may come to you without shame.

—Prayer translated by Chief Yellow Lark, Lakota, 1887

"THIS PICTURE illustrates the general character of the Sioux country. The broad rolling prairie is broken by low hills, while here and there lie pools of stagnant water in old buffalo-wallows. The subjects of the pictures are Red Hawk, Crazy Thunder and Holy Skin, three Oglala who accompanied the author on a trip into the Bad Lands." —ESC

"Friendship is held to be the severest test of character. It is easy, we think, to be loyal to family and clan, whose blood is in our own veins. . . . But to have a friend, and to be true under any and all trials, is the mark of a man!"

—Ohiyesa (Charles Eastman), Santee Dakota

In the Land of the Sioux, 1905

The Sioux, 1907

My horse be swift in flight
Even like a bird.
My horse be swift in flight
Bear me now in safety
Far from my enemy's arrows
And you shall be rewarded
With streamers and ribbons red.

—*Dakota Warrior's Song to his Horse*

"THIS PICTURE was made in the heart of the Bad Lands of South Dakota. The subject is the sub-chief Red Hawk. . . . Born in 1854. First war-party in 1865 under Crazy Horse, against troops. Led an unsuccessful war-party at twenty-two against Shoshoni. Engaged in twenty battles, many with troops, among them the Custer fight of 1876." —ESC

Grandfather, Great Spirit, once more behold me on earth and lean to hear my feeble voice. You lived first, and you are older than all need, older than all prayer. All things belong to you—the two-leggeds, the four-leggeds, the wings of the air and all green things that live. You have set the powers of the four quarters to cross each other. The good road and the road of difficulties you have made to cross; and where they cross, the place is holy. Day in and day out, forever, you are the life of all things.

—Black Elk, Oglala Lakota

Oasis in the Badlands, 1905

X 1452 - 05

Sioux Chiefs, 1905

In any great undertaking
it is not enough for a man
to depend simply upon himself.

—Lone Man

"THIS PICTURE was made on the Pine Ridge reservation in South Dakota at a time when the Indians were assembled in a large encampment, reliving the days of old." —ESC

In order to honor
[the Great Spirit],
I must honor
His works in Nature.

—Lakota wisdom

Prairie Chief. 1907

A River Camp—Yanktonai, 1908

The tipi is much better to live in;
always clean, warm in winter,
cool in summer, easy to move. . . .
If the Great Spirit wanted men to stay in one place
He would make the world stand still,
but He made it to always change . . . so birds and animals can move
and always have green grass and ripe berries,
sunlight to work and play, and night to sleep,
summer for flowers to bloom
and winter for them to sleep,
always changing everything for good.

—Flying Hawk, Oglala Lakota

"AS A RULE THE WOMEN OF THE PLAINS TRIBE are natural horsewomen, and their skill in riding is scarcely exceeded by that of the men. As mere infants they are tied upon the backs of trusty animals and thus become accustomed to the long days of journeying." —ESC

"Let me wish
the day's sunshine
may enter your soul."

—Zitkala Sa, Yanktonai Nakota

Daughters of a Chief, 1907

The Sioux Child, 1905

Grown men may learn from very little children,
for the hearts of little children are pure
and therefore, the Great Spirit
may show to them many things
which older people miss.

—Black Elk, Oglala Lakota

"A YOUNG SIOUX WOMAN in a dress made entirely of deerskin, embroidered with beads and porcupine quills." —ESC

Wakan'tanka
When I pray to him,
Hears me.
Whatever is good he
Grants me.

—Lakota song

Sioux Girl, 1907

x2587-07

Prayer to the Mystery, 1907

"IN SUPPLICATION THE PIPE was always offered to the Mystery by holding it aloft. At the feet of the worshipper lies a buffalo skull, symbolic of the spirit of the animal upon which the Indians were so dependent. The subject of the picture is Picket Pin, an Ogalala Sioux." —ESC

All these peoples, and all the things of the universe are joined to you who smoke the pipe. All send their voices to Wakan-Tanka, the Great Spirit. When you pray with this pipe, you pray for and with everything.

—Black Elk, Oglala Lakota

"SCATTERED THROUGHOUT THE INDIAN COUNTRY are found spots that are virtually shrines. These are often boulders or other rocks which through some chance have been invested with mythic significance, and to them priest and war-leaders repair to invoke the aid of supernatural powers. The half-buried bowlder [sic] on which the suppliant stands is accredited with the power of revealing to the warrior the foreordained result of his projected raid. Its surface bears what the Indians call the imprint of human feet, and it is owing to this peculiarity that it became a shrine. About it the soil is almost completely worn away by the generations of suppliants who have journeyed hither for divine revelation." —ESC

Hear me, four quarters of the world—a relative I am! Give me strength to walk the soft earth, a relative to all that is! Give me the eyes to see and the strength to understand, that I may be like you. With your power only can I face the winds.

—Black Elk, Oglala Lakota

Invocation — Sioux, 1907

High Hawk, 1907

"THE SUBJECT is shown in all the finery of a warrior dressed for a gala occasion—scalp-shirt, leggings, moccasins, and pipe-bag, all embroidered with porcupine-quills; eagle-feather war bonnet, and stone-headed war-club from the handle of which dangles a scalp. High Hawk is prominent among the Brules mainly because he is now their leading historical authority, being much in demand to determine the dates of events important to his fellow tribesmen." —ESC

Grandfather,
Look at our brokenness.
We know that in all creation
Only the human family
Has strayed from the Sacred Way.
We know that we are the ones
Who are divided.
And we are the ones
Who must come back together
To walk in the Sacred Way.

Grandfather,
Sacred one,
Teach us love, compassion, and honor
That we may heal the earth
and heal each other.

—Black Elk, Oglala Lakota

ONE OF THE WITTIEST AND SHREWDEST OF THE SIOUX CHIEFS was American Horse, who succeeded to the name and position of an uncle, killed in the Battle of Slim Buttes in 1876.... He had been tutored by his uncle, since his own father was killed in battle while he was still very young. —Charles Eastman (Ohiyesa), Santee Dakota

---

We will be known forever
by the tracks we leave.

—Dakota wisdom

American Horse, 1908

Slow Bull, 1907

Speak the truth in humility to all people.
Only then can you be a true man. . . .

—Lakota wisdom

Look at me, I am poor and naked, but I am the chief of the nation. We do not want riches, but we want to train our children right. Riches would do us no good. We could not take them with us to the other world. We do not want riches. We want peace and love.

—Mahpiua Luta (Red Cloud), Oglala Lakota

"Let us put our minds together and see what life we can make for our children."

—Tatanka Iyotanka (Sitting Bull),
   Hunkpapa Lakota

Red Cloud, 1905

Last Home of Joseph, 1905

The
NEZ PERCE

Chief Joseph, 1903

Tell General Howard I know his heart. What he told me before, I have in my heart. I am tired of fighting. Our chiefs are killed. Looking Glass is dead. Toohoolhoolzote is dead. The old men are all dead. It is the young men who say yes or no. He who led the young men is dead. It is cold and we have no blankets. The little children are freezing to death.

My people, some of them, have run away to the hills and have no blankets, no food. No one knows where they are—perhaps freezing to death. I want to have time to look for my children and see how many of them I can find. Maybe I shall find them among the dead.

Hear me, my chiefs! I am tired. My heart is sick and sad. From where the sun now stands I will fight no more forever.

—Chief Joseph, Nez Perce

I hope that no more groans of wounded
men and women will ever go to the ear of
the Great Spirit Chief above, and that all
people may be one people.

—Chief Joseph, Nez Perce

Joseph, 1903

Nez Perce Brave, 1905

It does not require many words to speak the truth.

—Chief Joseph, Nez Perce

Treat all men alike.

Give them all the same law.

Give them an even chance to live and grow.

All men are made by the same Great Spirit Chief.

They are all brothers.

—Chief Joseph, Nez Perce

The Old-Time Warrior, 1910

Nez Perce Matron, 1910

Nez Perce Babe, 1900

Three Eagles, 1910

We were taught to believe that the Great Spirit sees
and hears everything, and that he never forgets; that hereafter
he will give a man his spirit-home according to his deserts:
If he has been a good man, he will have a good home;
If he has been a bad man; he will have a bad home.
This I believe, and all my people believe the same.

—Chief Joseph, Nez Perce

Our fathers gave us many laws, which they had learned from their fathers. These laws were good. They told us to treat all men as they treated us; that we should never be first to break a bargain; that it was a disgrace to tell a lie; that we should speak only the truth . . .

—Chief Joseph, Nez Perce

Grizzly-Bear Ferocious, 1910

War Chief, 1905

Let me be a free man—free to travel, free to stop, free to work, free to trade where I choose, free to choose my own teachers, free to follow the religion of my fathers, free to think and talk and act for myself—and I will obey every law or submit to the penalty.

—Chief Joseph, Nez Perce

The earth is the mother of all people, and all people should have equal rights upon it. You might as well expect the rivers to run backward as that any man who was born a free man should be contented when penned up and denied liberty to go where he pleases.

—Chief Joseph, Nez Perce

BIBLIOGRAPHY

Aastrov, Margaret. *The Winged Serpent*. Greenwich, CT: Fawcett Publishing, 1975.

Babcock, Martin C., ed. *Walk Quietly The Beautiful Trail*. Kansas City: MO. Hallmark, 1973.

Baldwin, Gordon C. *Indians of the Southwest*. New York: Putnam, 1979.

Bierhorst, John, ed. *The Sacred Path: Spells, Prayers & Power Songs of the American Indians,* New York: Quill, 1984.

———. *In The Trail of the Wind: American Indian Poems and Ritual Orations*. New York: Farrar, Straus and Giroux, 1998.

Billard, Jules B., ed. *The World of The American Indian*. Washington, DC: National Geographic Society, 1979.

Brandon, William, ed. *The Magic World: American Indian Songs and Poems*. Athens, OH: Ohio University Press, 1991.

Brown, Joseph Epes, ed, *The Sacred Pipe: Black Elk's Account of the Seven Rites*

of the Oglala Sioux. Norman, OK: University of Oklahoma Press, 1989

Bunzel, Ruth L. "Zuni Ritual Poetry." *47th Annual Report Of The Bureau Of American Ethnology* 1929–1930, Washington, DC: Smithsonian Institution, 1932.

Cronyn, George W., ed. *American Indian Poetry: An Anthology of Songs and Chants.* New York: Fawcett Columbine, 1962.

Curtis, Edward S. *The North American Indian.* Cambridge, MA: Cambridge University Press, 1907–1930.

Curtis, Natalie. *The Indian's Book: Authentic Native American Legends, Lore and Music.* New York: Bonanza Books, 1987.

Day, A. Grove. *The Sky Clears: Poetry of The American Indians.* Lincoln, NE: University of Nebraska Press, 1964.

Densmore, Frances. *Nootka and Quileute Music.* Washington, DC: Government Printing Office, 1939.

———. *Teton Sioux Music and Culture.* Lincoln, NE: University of Nebraska Press, 1992.

Eastman, Charles A. *The Soul of The Indian: An Interpretation.* Boston: Houghton, 1911.

Editors of Time-Life Books. *The Spirit World.* Alexandria, VA: Time-Life Books, 1992.

———. *People of the Desert.* Alexandria, VA: Time-Life Books, 1993.

Egan, Timothy. *Short Nights of the Shadow Catcher: The Epic Life and Immortal Photographs of Edward S. Curtis.* Boston: Mariner Books, 2013.

Fitzgerald, Michael & Judith, eds. *The Spirit Of Indian Women.* Bloomington, IN: World Wisdom, 2005.

Graybill, Florence Curtis, and Victor Boesen. *Edward Sheriff Curtis: Visions of a Vanishing Race.* Boston: Houghton Mifflin, 1986.

Joe, Eugene Baatsoslanii, and Mark Bahti. *Navajo Sandpainting Art.* Tucson, AZ: Treasure Chest Publications, 1979.

Joseph, Nez Percé Chief. *Chief Joseph's Own Story.* Fairfield, WA: Ye Galleon Press, 1984.

Kawano, Kenji, and Benis M. Frank. *Warriors: Navajo Code Talkers.* Flagstaff, AZ: Northland, 1990.

Matthews, Washington. *The Night Chant: A Navaho Ceremony*, Salt Lake City: University of Utah Press, 1995.

McCreight, M. I. *Firewater and Forked Tongues: A Sioux Chief Interprets U.S. History.* Pasadena, CA: Trail's End Publishing, 1947.

McLuhan, T. C. *Touch The Earth: A Self-Portrait of Indian Existence.* New York: Outerbridge & Dienstfrey, 1971.

Neihardt, John G. *Black Elk Speaks.* Lincoln, NE: University of Nebraska Press, 1961.

Nerburn, Kent, and Louise Mengelkoch, eds. *Native American Wisdom.* San Rafael, CA: New World Library, 1991.

Powers, Willow Roberts. *Navajo Trading: The End Of An Era.* Albuquerque, NM: University of New Mexico Press, 2001.

Regier, Willis G., ed. *Masterpieces of American Indian Literature,* New York: MJF Books, 1993.

Speroff, Leon. *Carlos Montezuma M.D.: A Yavapai American Hero.* Portland, OR: Arnica Press, 2003.

Spinden, Herbert Joseph. *Songs of the Tewa.* New York: Exposition of Indian Tribal Arts, 1933.

Standing Bear, Luther. *Land of the Spotted Eagle.* Lincoln, NE: University of Nebraska Press, 1978.

Streep, Peg, ed. *The Sacred Journey: Prayers and Songs of Native America.* Boston: Bullfinch Press and Toronto: Little, Brown and Company, 1995.

Trimble, Stephen. *The People: Indians of the American Southwest.* Santa Fe, NM: School of American Research, 1995.

Underhill, Ruth M. *The Navajos.* Norman, OK: University of Oklahoma Press, 1956.

Wheelwright, Mary C. *Navajo Creation Myth: The Story of the Emergence, by Hasteen Klah.* Santa Fe, NM: Museum of Ceremonial Art, 1942.

White Lance, Francis. *Tasunke Witko Woihanble: The Vision of Crazy Horse.* CreateSpace, 2012.

I want to teach my people
to hold on to the future
with all of our strength.

—Manuelito, Navajo chief

PHOTO CREDITS